Daisy's Adventures
Lesson Plans
For Set #1

Wynter Sommers

United States

Copyright © 2017 Susan E. dePillis and G.J. dePillis

Library of Congress Control Number: 2018943526

Published by Pure Force Enterprises, Inc.
California, USA
Since 2002

INGRAM
INGRAM® Distribution

All rights reserved. No part of this book may be used or reproduced by any means, including and not limited to graphic, electronic, or mechanical, including photocopying, recording, taping or by any information storage retrieval system without the written permission of the authors except in the case of brief quotations embodied in critical articles and reviews.

This novel is a work of fiction. Names, places, characters, and incidents are either the product of the author's imagination or, if real, are used fictitiously.

ISBN-13: 978-1-7184-0001-6
ISBN-10: 1-7184-0001-2

TABLE OF CONTENTS

Introduction to Nine Titles of Daisy's Adventures...... 1

1 Daisy's Story...3

2 Daisy's Independence Day Picnic...............................5

3 Daisy's Special Date...7

4 Daisy's Homework...9

5 Daisy's Parrot...11

6 Daisy and the Gerry..13

7 Daisy and the Facts...15

8 Daisy's Ice Cream Garden..18

9 Daisy's White House...21

10 Lesson Plan Supplement..23

11 ISBNs & Bar Codes..30

<u>NOTE:</u> For Lesson Plan Supplement ACTIVITIES, see pages 25 through 30.

NOTICE

These lesson plans are designed to support the 9 titles found in Set #1 of Daisy's Adventures.

Thank you for incorporating Daisy's Adventures into your education program.

We hope you enjoy the added dimension of support which this series of fictional adventures brings to WWII United States History and social studies.

Enjoy!

Daisy's Adventures Lesson Plans For Set #1 by Wynter Sommers

Introduction to Nine Titles of Daisy's Adventures

Theme:

<u>Daisy's Adventures</u> is a set of 9 individual titles about a young orphan living in the USA during WWII.

Vocabulary:

Orphan- An orphan is a child who has no mother, father or family to care for her or him.

Orphanage A place set up by adults to take care of orphans. An orphanage has a school, bedrooms for sleeping, dining room for meals, daily schedule of activities organized and administered by professional adults, etc.

WWII "World War Two" In the year 1933, Adolf Hitler became the leader of Germany. His group was called National Socialists (the NAZI party). In 1938 Hitler led the Germans to take the country of Austria claiming that Germany needed "living space." Other countries joined Hitler. They were called the AXIS which included Germany, Italy, and Japan. They attacked many countries such as Poland. Russia cooperated with the AXIS. Other nations around the world were angry at the AXIS group. Nations such as England and France were called the ALLIES.

Daisy's Adventures Lesson Plans For Set #1 by Wynter Sommers

In 1941 people were surprised when Germany attacked Russia. So Russia turned against the AXIS and began to help the ALLIES.

The ALLIES wanted the USA to join them, but the USA had already helped these countries to win WWI. (World War One). The USA now wanted peace to study Science, make inventions, grow food, build roads, houses, and bridges.

The USA became angry and joined the ALLIES on December 7, 1941 when Japan dropped bombs on Pearl Harbor, Hawaii. Finally, World War Two (WWII) ended when the AXIS surrendered to the ALLIES in 1945.

Treasure...A treasure is something which is much desired. It can be jewelry, minerals such as gold or silver, or a person who is loved.

Adopt/ adoption- To adopt is to take into a new relationship. To raise as one's own.

This is a SET of Lesson Plans. There is one lesson plan per Daisy's Adventures story. This book is an introduction to the collection (or BUNDLED SET) of 9 individual titles together.

The following Lesson Plans (1 through 9) address each separate title of **Daisy's Adventures Set #1.**

1 Daisy's Story
Lesson Plan 1

(ISBN- 13) 978-0-9791080-1-3

Theme:

Daisy grew up in an orphanage in the USA during WWII. She dreamed about the most wonderful of all treasures, belonging to a family of her very own. But, no matter how hard she tried, Daisy was always passed over for adoption. And then one day...

Vocabulary:

Prospect   A future hope.

Trustees/Governing Board... People who run an organization, usually adults.

Chicken coop...A small place to keep chickens outside.

Down/ downy...The soft feathers of a tiny chick.

Ration/rationing... A ration is only a small part of a large supply. If the usual amount of bread is four slices, the bread ration is one slice.

The Great War... World War I started in 1914. It ended November 11, 1918.

WWII... World War II started in the year 1939. It ended in 1945.

Banish... Chase away.

Mimic... To copy the actions or speech of someone or something else.

Ponder... To think about something very carefully, sometimes for a long while.

Succumb... To give up.

Potential... Anything that is possible, but not real yet.

Comportment... The way a person behaves. Manners.

Portfolio... A box or bag for carrying important papers.

The above is Lesson Plan 1.
The following Lesson Plans (2 through 9) address other titles of **Daisy's Advent**

2 Daisy's Independence Day Picnic
Lesson Plan 2

(ISBN-13) 978-0-9791080-2-0

Theme:

Daisy and her newly adopted Mother are on their first family outing at a July 4th picnic hosted by the Bide-A-While orphanage. Daisy had lived at the Bide-A-While all her life before being adopted.

Daisy happily greets many familiar friends from the orphanage who are there with their own newly adopted families.

Then Daisy meets someone she has never seen before, someone who may change her life, yet again...

Vocabulary:

Chiffon...A sheer fabric of silk or nylon.

Comment... To talk about something, or to explain.

Perplex/perplexed... To be perplexed is to be confused, puzzled, to be mixed up.

Instruction manual... A book telling the reader how to do a job or fix something.

Presentable...Wearing suitable, proper clothing to meet company.

Mathematician...A scientist who examines patterns and discovers universal relationships.

The above is Lesson Plan 2.

The following Lesson Plans (3 through 9) each address a separate title of Daisy's Adventures.

3 Daisy's Special Date
Lesson Plan 3

(ISBN -13) 978-0-9791080-3-7

Theme:

Daisy wants to surprise her newly adopted Mother on this special date, Mother's birthday. It is the first birthday Mother has celebrated since Daisy's adoption. Daisy wants to bake a beautiful cake, but her plans are foiled by WWII sugar rationing. Daisy has to be creative and resourceful, but will she be able to present Mother with a wonderful surprise, or will it be Daisy who gets surprised?

Vocabulary:

Squint/ squinting...To look at something with half-closed eyes, as if looking into a bright light.

Foreign... Outside of one's own country or location. It is foreign when it is in a place where it is not usually found.

Statistics... A part of mathematics which gathers and studies large collections of facts and information.

Bureau...1) A bureau is a government or business office or department with special information or service such as "travel bureau". 2) Furniture with drawers for clothing.

Recipe...A list of foods and directions for making something special to eat

Announce... To say something loudly enough for many people to hear.

Admonish... To scold or warn gently.

Determination... A firm strong promise to get something done.

Grit...Firmness of spirit and character. Staying with something until it is done right.

Humorous... Comical; making a person or people laugh.

Articulate... To say words or explain ideas so they are clear and easy to understand.

This above is Lesson Plan 3.
The following Lesson Plans (4 through 9) address additional individual titles about ***Daisy's Adventures***.

4 Daisy's Homework Lesson Plan 4

(ISBN-13) 978-0-9791080-4-4

Theme:

Daisy returns home after school feeling sad, discouraged and overwhelmed by her homework assignment. Her perspective changes as she sees how her own skills blend together into something wonderful, but only if Daisy minds each step along the way. Will she? Can she?

Vocabulary:

Textbooks...The main words of written or printed information in a book, but not separate notes or even indexes, illustrations, separate commentary. Text books are usually used as part of school and classroom instruction.

Assignment...Follow up activity from a classroom lesson, usually given by a teacher to classroom students. Assignments are generally given a special length of time in which to be completed.

Admire...To look at with approval, wonder, and general agreement.

Incident...Something that takes place or happens. An event or action.

Intervention...The act of coming between two or more situations. Move in between the actions of others in order to change what is happening.

Impoverished... Very poor, with few resources.

Big Ben...This is a clock tower in Westminster Palace, London, England. It was named for Sir Benjamin Hall who, as Commissioner of Works, had it put up in 1856. It has 4 clock faces. It is 315 feet tall, has 334 steps to get to the belfry, and 399 steps to the top of the tower. The bell weighs 13 tons.

✪ The math problem is explained in Chapter 5 starting on Page 27 of *Daisy's Homework*.

The above is Lesson Plan 4

The following Lesson Plans (5 through 9) address more titles of **Daisy's Adventures**.

5 Daisy's Parrot
Lesson Plan 5

(ISBN-13) 978-0-9791080-5-1

Theme:

Daisy, and her newly adopted Mother, visit Mother's friend for lunch. There they meet other guests, and find a parrot sitting on the shoulder of one of the visitors. Daisy and Mother hear how the parrot may have a very different meaning to these guests than what Daisy and Mother possibly expected. Daisy even learns that parrots have saved the lives of pilots flying in the WWII USA military Air Force. How could parrots help the military of the USA?

Vocabulary:

Grudgingly... To unwillingly agree with a comment or decision, etc. that has been made by someone else.

Foyer...An entrance hall in a large home, or in a theater.

Apologize... To say or write that you are sorry for having done something.

Glance... 1) To look at something quickly and then look away. 2) Something hits another object at an angle and then bounces (glances) off.

Species...A group of individuals or objects having similar appearance, behavior, or characteristics, and is usually called by a common name.

Poster...A large printed sheet of paper which is put up on a wall to give public information, announcements, advertising. A bill, a notice, a placard.

Shell Shock...The term "shell" referred to the casing of a bomb or explosive and was first used in the military around 1640. It refers to the hollow object filled with explosives. The psychological damage from the explosion was first recorded around 1915, hence came the term "shell shock" to refer to a battle weary soldier who was stunned by explosives.

The above is Lesson Plan 5.
The following Lesson Plans (6 through 9) address more titles of *Daisy's Adventures*.

6 Daisy and the Gerry Lesson Plan 6

(ISBN-13) 978-0-9791080-9-9

Theme:

Daisy's Teacher sets up a classroom game about American history. Daisy thinks the lesson will be boring, but she suddenly pays attention when Teacher begins to talk about something called "gerrymandering".

During the lesson, students try to untangle ideas about redrawing districts, voting, and deciding who gets cookies.

Will Daisy and her friends in class be able to explain "gerrymandering" to their parents before the grown-ups head out to the polls?

Vocabulary:

Pop Quiz... This is a set of questions, or a test, given by surprise to students in class. Students have not been told in advance about the test, so they have not had extra time to study for it.

Groan/ groaned... A low sound made in the throat to express pain, sadness, disappointment.

Murmur/ murmured... Words which are spoken by one or by several people at once. The words are not said clearly and are uttered in low voices.

Commend/ commended... To praise. To tell someone they are right and have done well.

Deprive... To take something away from someone. To stop someone from having or getting something they need.

Ignore... To pretend you do not hear or see something that is there.

Indicate... To point to an object that someone else may not have seen. To explain or say something about a situation or idea or thing that others may have overlooked.

The above is Lesson Plan 6.
The following Lesson Plans (7 through 9) address additional titles of *Daisy's Adventures*.

7 Daisy and the Facts Lesson Plan 7

(ISBN-13) 978-0-9791080-7-5

Theme:

Daisy becomes the target of false gossip at school. She does not understand how this could have happened, or why. She shares her sadness with her adopted Mother. After listening carefully to Daisy, Mother explains that whole groups of people, even entire populations, can be tricked into believing a lie. Mother explains that the USA is fighting World War II against an enemy who is clever at spreading lies.

When lies are made up and spread by the enemy, good people may believe the lies and stop looking for the truth. When good people stop looking for the facts and stop searching for the truth, they are vulnerable for a takeover by the very enemy who wants to destroy them.

Will Daisy be able to get the facts? Will she be able to stop the lies and share the truth?

Vocabulary:

Pout/ pouting...To frown and push your lips out or down to show you are upset or annoyed.

Gossip...To talk, and even tell lies, about another person's behavior and life. A person who gossips likes to spread stories, personal details, and lies about another individual to as many people as is possible. The gossip wants to control the way other people treat the individual the gossip is lying about.

Obvious... An object or idea is obvious when it is easy to see and/or is clearly understood.

Exhausted... To be exhausted is to be very, very tired.

Verify... To verify a statement or report is to prove something has really happened. To verify is to get the facts and show that what has been said, or done, has truly been seen and reported by people, circumstances, scientific proof or other honest means of showing the truth.

Indignant... To be indignant is to be upset, displeased, very annoyed.

Malicious... To be malicious is to be hateful, to do things you know will hurt innocent people. To be spiteful.

Succumb/ succumbing...To succumb to someone (or something) is to stop fighting against.

Propaganda ... This word has been in use since 1718. It refers to a way to replicate or propagate or spread an idea or concept so people will believe it. It was used in common language around World War I. It was a term used when one group tried to convince another group to change their political beliefs and actions. It was used as a term "to advance a cause" around 1929.

The above is Lesson Plan 7.

The following Lesson Plans (8 through 9) address additional titles of *Daisy's Adventures*.

8 Daisy's Ice Cream Garden Lesson Plan 8

(ISBN-13) 978-0-9791080-8-2

Theme:

Daisy and her friends, James and Minnie, investigate a garden plot which James' adopted parents have surprised them all by renting. Daisy, Minnie, and James are amazed to learn they will be able to get a lot of food for each of their adopted families, without having to go to the grocery store or vegetable market with ration books. They find they can get much more food to eat beyond their rationed supplies. But what happens when they try to work as a team? And what is the real meaning of friendship and selflessness?

Vocabulary:

Dismiss/ dismissed... To be told to leave a place or area, such as being dismissed from a classroom or from school. To be dispersed or removed.

Chauffeur...A chauffeur is a person hired (paid) to drive a car for someone else.

Community...A community is made of a group of people who live near each other in one area, agree to the same laws, have the same interests. A village, a colony, a hamlet. The people who live in the same community can agree to set up an activity which they all will support, such as a "community garden", a "community theater", a "community market".

Groundskeeper/ groundskeepers... A person, or group of people, paid to take care of the land (or grounds) around someone's house or estate. Groundskeepers (also called "gardeners") trim trees, take away weeds, care for the vegetables and fruits and flowers, and generally do what is needed to keep the "grounds" looking nice.

Vehicle...A vehicle is a car or truck or bus or wagon or anything which can move from place to place while carrying people. Any device for transporting people or things.

Contagious...A person is said to be contagious when something like a virus or bacteria moves from that person (who is sick with a disease) to another person who is not sick. The person who was not sick becomes sick from the person who spread the contagious disease. Related words are: Communicable, epidemic, spreading by contact.

Extract/ extracted...To extract is to pull something out from where it was. You can extract a toy from a gift box. You can squeeze an orange to extract juice from inside.

Victory Garden...This was a garden one would grow at home or in a "community garden" to harvest vegetables in order to augment the food rations allotted to each civilian during WWII. It was first used around 1940.

Emolument...Payment for doing a job or service.

The above is Lesson Plan 8.

The following Lesson Plan (9) addresses another of *Daisy's Adventures*.

9 Daisy's White House Lesson Plan 9

(ISBN-13) 978-0-9791080-6-8

Theme:

Daisy learns the hard way about confidence tricksters. She also learns how people of good character were needed, required, in the founding of the United States of America (USA). Although she thought her excursion with her adopted Mother would probably be tiresome, she loved being with Mother and so wanted to come along.

But what did she find out about the symbols on the paper money used in the USA? And what was happening to soldiers of the USA during that special time?

Vocabulary:

Wince/ winced...To wince is to suddenly pull back and away from something. To flinch, to recoil, to twitch, to cringe.

Tour...A tour is an excursion or trip to see the outsides and/or insides of special buildings, cities, and other areas. When you go on a tour, you follow a plan for a particular period of time in order to explore locations which are unfamiliar.

Fashion/ fashionable...To follow fashion, or to be fashionable, is to wear clothing and other items which are currently popular. The prevailing style or mode. The custom or practice which most people agree is popular.

Vendor... A vendor is a person, or an organized group of people, who make or buy things to sell to other people.

Chuckle/ chuckled... To chuckle is to laugh softly, gently.

Souvenir...A souvenir is a simple object, or small token, brought from a special place to help you to remember your visit.

The above is Lesson Plan 9.
When you order the bundle, you get all 9 titles in the complete ***Daisy's Adventures Set #1***

10 Lesson Plan Supplement

SUPPLEMENT
This is a SUPPLEMENT to the foregoing Lesson Plans for the nine individual titles of DAISY'S ADVENTURES.

The SUPPLEMENT provides additional instructor options for:
- DISCUSSION IDEAS
- GROUP PROJECTS
- INDEPENDENT ASSIGNMENTS
- RESEARCH

CONTENTS
DAISY'S ADVENTURES contain the nine following titles.
    (1) Daisy's Story
    (2) Daisy's Independence Picnic
    (3) Daisy's Special Date
    (4) Daisy's Homework
    (5) Daisy's Parrot
    (6) Daisy and the Gerry
    (7) Daisy and the Facts
    (8) Daisy's Ice Cream Garden
    (9) Daisy's White House

OBJECTIVES
    Provide introductory background information about World War Two (WWII), and refer to World War One (WWI).

  . Historical examination of democratic governments (ALLIES in WWII) versus authoritarian governments (AXIS in WWII).

Civics exploration of the process of forming a government including the process of voting, enfranchisement, disenfranchisement, limits of government power, taking over a government by force to restrict or eliminate citizen participation.

Social consequences of living in a democracy vs.under an authoritarian system for individuals and groups of people. What happens when people come from varying cultures, beliefs, traditions, ethnicities, experiences? Would there be expanded or severely limited opportunities to develop one's talent, get the best education, earn a living, locate a place in which to live, secure health care, receive help in case of natural or man-made disasters (storms, fires, floods, earthquakes, and other harmful situations).

PREPARATION (10 minutes)
Distribute the vocabulary list (photocopy or display or write the words on a board for the class to see)

LESSON (15-20 Minutes): Introduce **DAISY'S ADVENTURES** to the students by explaining they will learn vocabulary and then read the text of the book. We will only read the first part of Chapter 1. One teacher option can be to read aloud to the class. With another option, instructor determines how long students shall read silently to themselves.

Review the vocabulary appropriate for this lesson.
    1) Use the vocabulary they learned. Ask them to give examples of other sentences which use that word.
    2) Inform them that talking about the topic in general and understanding the vocabulary makes them stronger readers and better analysts

3) Explain to students they may need to read the text a few times and then discuss it with a partner.

ACTIVITY (15 minutes)
Ask the children to read quietly to themselves.
Ask the children to pair up and discuss the Daisy character with a partner. How old do you think she is? What does she look like? Is she friendly? Is she kind? Helpful?
1) Do you think Daisy's situation in the 1940's could happen in the USA today? Why or why not
2) What do you think will happen next in the story?

REVIEW and CLOSE (15 minutes)
Ask a pair of students to share what they discussed and what the first part of the story means in today's world versus the USA in the world of WWII.

HOMEWORK & Questions to ask when the book has been fully read by the student. Discussion could last a full class period. Length of discussion is at teacher's discretion.
  Option: Remind students to read the rest of the text on their own time at home. When they return to class, you will continue the discussion about the story.
1) Which character do you identify with the most? Which do you identify with the least? Why?
2) What was happening in the world during the 1940's? What was happening specifically in the United States in the 1940's? Why did the United States join the war? Ask students to back up answers with historical examples.
3) What was American culture like at that time?
4) How were schools different, then versus now?

5) How were orphanages different during WWII versus now?

6) Was the government of the USA run differently or the same comparing then versus now?

7) Instead of just memorizing historical facts and dates, put some meaning behind them. Ask students to find a fresh source of research material to prove their facts are true (corroboration of source material). Through class discussion, check for understanding regarding the context in which an event happened.

- Describe one specific event and what triggered that event.
- How were civilian disagreements resolved in the USA during WWII? Are there similar triggers to conflicts building in our society today?
- Ask students what they think Daisy and the other characters felt during that time?
- Do students believe people today would feel the same way under similar circumstances? Ask students how they or other people would react?
- Ask students for their opinion as to whether the response in Daisy's situation was a good response? Why and why not?
- Ask students if they could summarize a Daisy story in a sentence or two.
- Using, **Daisy and the Gerry**, do the students feel they understand gerrymandering enough to explain it to a grown-up? How would they explain it?
- Using **Daisy's Parrot**, do the students feel "shell shock" and PTSD (Post Traumatic Stress Disorder) are the same? How would therapy via service comfort animals help with healing?

FINAL SHOWCASE

When the reading assignment has been completed for a specific Daisy book, and discussion questions have been assigned and completed, encourage students to share their findings after researching the era of the Daisy stories (1940's USA).

After reading a Daisy book and submitting written responses to classroom questions, students should demonstrate an understanding of the historic era, plot comprehension, and vocabulary.

CULMINATION

To support student efforts, their "extra credit" work should be "showcased" by displaying it in a manner which conveys approval.

"You did a bit extra. It was a job well done".

Make a comment on the creativity which students demonstrated when they shared their understanding of the subject matter.

It is important for the student to demonstrate understanding of the structured facts of their research and how those techniques can be applied to any subject.

1. Observe the phenomenon
2. Identify the root cause of the problem
3. Gather data
4. Hypothesize (find a pattern in your data)
5. Test the hypothesis

Example:
1. Observe the bubbles in a pot of (boiling) water.

2. Identify the heat source under the pot

3. Measure the temperature of unheated water. As the water heats up, keep measuring the temperature and log the data at regular intervals. At what temperature does the water finally start to bubble (boil)?

4. Hypothesize that water needs to reach a temperature of 212°F (100°C) in order to bubble (boil).

5. Repeat the experiment to see if the water starts to bubble (boil) at a different temperature than 212°F (100°C)

Thank students for their positive contributions to the class and understanding of Daisy's world.

ABOUT THE AUTHOR

Wynter Sommers is the pseudonym for an American writing team. One is a technology specialist. The other has thirty years of experience applying her PhD in Education to teach classrooms of enthusiastic students. Both have a heart to inspire creativity in children, encourage supportive family bonds, and share information and observations about life as it was in America during WWII.

Wynter Sommers hopes you will enjoy the other DAISY'S ADVENTURES stories in this series.

11 ISBNs & Bar Codes

Daisy's Adventures Bundle for Set #1
ISBN(13)=978-1-7184-0000-9
ISBN(10)=1-7184-0000-4

- **Daisy's Story**
  ISBN(13) = 978-0-9791080-1-3
  ISBN(10) = 0-9791080-1-2
- **Daisy's Independence Picnic**
  ISBN(13) = 978-0-9791080-2-0
  ISBN(10) = 0-9791080-2-0
- **Daisy's Special Date**
  ISBN(13) = 978-0-9791080-3-7
  ISBN(10) = 0-9791080-3-9
- **Daisy's Homework**
  ISBN(13) = 978-0-9791080-4-4
  ISBN(10) = 0-9791080-4-7
- **Daisy's Parrot**
  ISBN(13) = 978-0-9791080-5-1
  ISBN(10) = 0-9791080-5-5
- **Daisy and the Gerry**
  ISBN(13) = 978-0-9791080-9-9
  ISBN(10) = 0-9791080-9-8
- **Daisy and the Facts**
  ISBN(13) = 978-0-9791080-7-5
  ISBN(10) = 0-9791080-7-1
- **Daisy's Ice Cream Garden**
  ISBN(13) = 978-0-9791080-8-2
  ISBN(10) = 0-9791080-1-2-8-x
- **Daisy's White House**
  ISBN(13) = 978-0-9791080-6-8
  ISBN(10) = 0-9791080-6-3
- **Daisy's Adventures Lesson Plans for Set #1**
  ISBN(13) = 978-1-7184-0001-6
  ISBN(10) = 1-7184-0001-2

Daisy's Adventures Lesson Plans For Set #1 by Wynter Sommers

1. Daisy's Story

ISBN 978-0-9791080-1-3

2. Daisy's Independence Picnic

ISBN 978-0-9791080-2-0

3. Daisy's Special Date

ISBN 978-0-9791080-3-7

4. Daisy's Homework

ISBN 978-0-9791080-4-4

Daisy's Adventures Lesson Plans For Set #1 by Wynter Sommers

Daisy's Parrot

ISBN 978-0-9791080-5-1

Daisy and the Gerry

ISBN 978-0-9791080-6-8

Daisy and the Facts

Daisy's Ice Cream Garden

ISBN 978-0-9791080-7-5

ISBN 978-0-9791080-8-2

Daisy's Adventures Lesson Plans For Set #1 by Wynter Sommers

 Daisy's White House

ISBN 978-0-9791080-9-9

 Daisy's Adventures Lesson Plans for Set #1

ISBN 978-1-7184-0001-6

Daisy' Adventures Bundle for Set #1
All 9 Daisy Books + Lesson Plans = 10 books
ISBN 978-1-7184-0000-9

www.ingramcontent.com/pod-product-compliance
Lightning Source LLC
Chambersburg PA
CBHW031227170426
43191CB00030B/304